Into the Desert

Into the Desert

Reflections for Lent

George Lacey, OSB

Paulist Press
New York/Mahwah, N.J.

Cover design by Sharyn Banks
Book design by Lynn Else

Library of Congress Cataloging-in-Publication Data

Lacey, George, 1932-
    Into the desert : reflections for Lent / George Lacey.
        p. cm.
    ISBN 0-8091-4283-X (alk. paper)
    1. Lent—Prayer-books and devotions—English. I. Title.

BX2170.L4L333 2004
242'.34—dc22

                                                    2004011041

Published by Paulist Press
997 Macarthur Boulevard
Mahwah, New Jersey 07430

www.paulistpress.com

Printed and bound in Canada

CONTENTS

FOREWORD

These reflections can be used in several ways. Some can be used as brief homilies at the daily Masses during Lent, since they are often loosely related to the readings. (The readings for Sundays follow year B.) They can also be used as readings for the daily Divine Office. Or they can be used for what they are primarily intended, that is, as daily reflections for the season of Lent.

Special thanks are due to J. and K. Byron for checking the scriptural references and making other valuable corrections of grammar and syntax.

ASH WEDNESDAY

I Hate Lent

"Remember that thou art dust, and unto dust thou shalt return," says the priest as he puts a dab of ash on your forehead on Ash Wednesday.

I use the somewhat archaic familiar form of the pronoun *you—thou—*since Lent is meant to get down deep and personal: "Thou art dust"; you, in particular are human. The word *human* is related to *humus,* earth. Indeed, the name Adam (according to Genesis, the first human) means *red soil.* Given our origin, a certain humility, also related to *humus,* is clearly in order.

Ash Wednesday also reminds us of our mortality: "And unto dust thou shalt return." Again, the *thou* is second person singular—getting down deep and personal. We came from dust, and, no matter the marvels of modern medicine, we will return to dust.

Amidst such sobering meditations we may wish the priest had used the alternative verse when placing ashes on our forehead: "Repent and believe in the gospel." We know from the experience of previous Lents that this is not a particularly upbeat topic either, for what we are to repent of is our sins. There are even patterns of sin. For sin, as we know, breeds sin. The lie we tell requires another to cover that one up, which needs another to conceal those two, and so on. We listen to gossip and cannot resist passing on the juicy tidbit, with garnish, to someone else. One can see sin breeding sin in the history of the church as well.

The sin that was the Inquisition was bred by the sin of the forced baptism of Jews in Spain.

Reflections on dust and ashes, humility and mortality, sin and repentance, are some of the reasons I hate Lent. It's all too depressing—straightening out one's life, turning it around, when the memory of past failed attempts of previous Lents are all too real.

However, there is also the other side to that alternative verse: "And believe in the gospel," the good news. And the good news is that Christ died for our sins and redeemed us from them. We may have doubts about our ability to get our lives turned around—and rightly so. However, we know that the Lord Jesus has not given up on us. After all, he has given us another Lent.

Even if I still hate it.

THURSDAY AFTER ASH WEDNESDAY

Choose Life

Choose life, says the book of Deuteronomy, describing it as better than the alternative.

Jesus did not choose death. Rather, he says to his disciples in today's gospel that the Son of Man will be put to death after being rejected by the elders, the high priests, and the scribes. So death was imposed upon him? Well, not quite. It was a death that he freely accepted. So he chose death? Again, not quite. He chose to do the will of the Father. And this choice involved his death.

Today, especially in relation to the terminally ill, we speak of the quality of life. And, what with the current state of health care, it is possible to continue a person's life beyond the point where it really has meaning as a life. If I am having a nightmare and do not like what is going on in the dream—say I'm being chased by muggers or falling off a tall building—I wake myself up. After all, it's my dream, and if I don't like it I can turn it off, like a bad television program. So if I'm irreversibly ill, with a rapidly deteriorating quality of life, in severe pain, am I permitted just to end it all, or have it ended in a doctor-assisted suicide?

"Those who find their life will lose it, and those who lose their life for my sake will find it" (Mt 10:39), says Jesus. Indeed, one can go to great expense with the latest in medical technologies and reach a point of diminishing returns when it comes to the quality of life. The principle from an older moral theology strikes me as still valid: one is not morally obliged to take extraordinary means to preserve one's life. One may quibble about what constitutes "extraordinary means"; however, the principle still retains its validity.

But there is also the other side of the sentence, "...whoever loses his life for my sake will save it." In the first place, Jesus speaks of "losing" one's own life, not "taking" it. Jesus did not take his own life: he was put to death, albeit a death he freely accepted. Also, Jesus speaks of "losing one's life *for his sake*," in the same way that he gave up his life for the sake of doing his Father's will. So can one say, "It's *my* life, and it has become a nightmare, and I'm ending it?" Indeed, it is my life, but it's not just mine. There are also others that have a claim upon it: family members, friends, associates, even those with whom we may have long been at enmity may need us to stay around long enough so that they can make their peace with us. And there is always God, the ultimate source of our life who may have an interest in our continuing to live at least a little longer so that there may be repentance and acceptance of his will on our part. In Gethsemane, Jesus says, ..."Not what I want, but what you want" (Mk 14:36).

It is only by losing our life for his sake, and on his terms, that we can expect to be given back a life better than the life we lose.

FRIDAY AFTER
ASH WEDNESDAY

Fasting

Fasting is associated with the world's major religions. This is certainly true of Judaism. In Islam, there is Ramadan. Buddhist monks eat only one meal a day.

The purpose of fasting is to strengthen the life of the spirit by weakening the desire for sensual pleasures. Not that the pleasures of food and drink are evil. To the contrary. They are recognized as goods given by God for our enjoyment as well as for the sustenance of our bodies. Nevertheless, forswearing such goods represents a way in which to indicate to our bodies that the life of the spirit is more important. One might say that in the same way that food nourishes the body, so fasting nourishes the soul.

Fasting is not the same as dieting. Taking off weight in order to fit into last summer's swimsuit is not a religious exercise. One can always buy a new, and larger, swimsuit. Similarly, going on a diet because the doctor tells us we need to lose weight in order to avoid serious health problems is not fasting. And obviously, fasting has nothing whatsoever to do with an eating disorder such as anorexia, in which one ends up, literally, starving oneself to death.

In chapter 49 of his Rule, "Regarding the Observance of Lent," St. Benedict speaks about denying oneself not only something in the way of food and drink but also sleep, needless talking, and idle jests. However, he insists that what we do for Lent should not be merely abstaining, giving up this or that, even though when it comes to evil habits this is a very good place to start. What Benedict urges especially are positive steps. Lent should be a time when we are more faithful to the duties of our state in life, perhaps even an increase in our accustomed service, above all in the matters of private prayer, holy reading and compunction of heart.

Though when it comes to compunction of heart and considering past sins, there is one piece of advice that should be followed: look, but don't stare. Acknowledging one's faults and failings is one thing, but dwelling on them may only produce more of the same. Also, meditating overmuch on the text "I am a worm and not human..." (Ps 22:6), while it may appear to excite feelings of "humility," can also undermine the true humility which recognizes the good that is in us, the good that God enables us to do.

Benedict also indicates the reason why we shouldn't hate Lent. It is an opportunity "to wash away in this holy season the negligences of past times." Thus, through the practices of Lent we may look forward to the joyful celebration of holy Easter, Jesus' rising from the dead, and our own rising to new life.

SATURDAY AFTER
ASH WEDNESDAY

Sinners

One thing universally attributed to Jesus in the gospels, and something for which he was abundantly condemned by the religious types of his time, was that he associated with sinners, with those who did not and, in some cases because of their occupation, could not observe the prescripts of the law. In his defense, Jesus insists that it is precisely sinners, those outside the law, who are in need of his healing ministry, in need of a change of heart, in need of conversion.

The physician treats those who are ill, not the healthy. Preventive medicine was not all that big in the ancient world, although Jesus has something to say along those lines as well. Murder is wrong, but avoid even the angry word (Mt 5:22). Adultery is wrong, but avoid even the lustful thought (Mt 5:28).

What is so bad about sin is that the person begins to die from the inside out. It is like root rot in a tree, like Alzheimer's disease in the brain. Part of a person just dies. And, unless somehow checked, it spreads. Root rot in one tree spreads to others in the forest. The religious teachers of Israel were well aware that when one area of the law is not observed, soon there will be other areas, and still others, that will be unkept. And before long, the law simply becomes irrelevant to one's life. This is why the rabbis set up hedges around the law, so as to make it difficult to get even close to the law's violation. Just like Jesus' insistence that even the angry word or the lustful thought is wrong.

Let us take the law of the new covenant, which may appropriately be understood as the law of love. Let's say we stop loving someone, a spouse, a confrere. We gradually—and it is a gradual process—cease doing the little things we know please the other person, we become less considerate of their feelings. Before long, there are words we regret saying. We eventually become irritated with their love for us, since we have fallen out of love with them. Their love becomes a reproach. The love that was once in our hearts has gone dead. Where there was love, now there is only emptiness, nothing.

Is it possible to revive a lost love, repair a broken relationship? As we know from experience, it is never easy. But is it possible? To be perfectly honest, from a purely human point of view, once the fire has completely gone out, it cannot be rekindled. Once the tree has died, watering a dead stump will not bring it back to life. Once Alzheimer's has fully set in, the person we knew is simply no longer there.

But all that is from a purely human point of view. Can God bring to life that which shows no signs of life? The prophet Isaiah says yes. The Lord can give you plenty even on a parched land, renew your strength, make you like a watered garden, like a spring whose waters never fail.

We may give up on the other person; we may have long since given up on ourselves. However, we should never give up on God and on his ability to revive a relationship, a life, a love that may have failed. After all, God raised his son who was crucified, dead, and buried. Something is permanently and finally dead only when God says it's dead. And he is the Lord of the living.

FIRST SUNDAY OF LENT

The Desert

The desert is a stark and austere place. It is a wasteland, a wilderness. Not much is living out there, just a few wild animals; that's about it. As today's gospel indicates, it is a stark and austere spiritual landscape as well. There are angels there ministering to Jesus in the wilderness. And there is Satan who has come out to test Jesus.

Mark does not indicate the content of the temptations to which Satan subjects Jesus. But one thing may be certain: they are genuine temptations. Like ours, the temptations are personally adjusted to the person; they probe the weak spots; they seek out the areas where there is softness.

Yet, sorely as we may be tempted away from the path of salvation we know that "we do not have a high priest who is unable to sympathize with our weaknesses, but we have one who in every respect has been tested as we are, yet without sin" (Heb 4:15).

It is clear that Jesus passed the test. For the next verses in Mark's Gospel indicate that Jesus begins his public ministry in Galilee, announcing the time of fulfillment, the proximity of the reign of God, the need to repent and to believe in the good news.

Jesus' time in the desert, in the wilderness, is not a period of rest before beginning the work of his public ministry. Rather, it is a time for getting some things out of the way, like the temptations of Satan. It is a time of preparation for what is to come, and thus above all a time of prayer, of communing with God. It is a time for strengthening, building up the spiritual reserves, before setting out on a journey. It is doubtful that Jesus could see as far as the end of the journey at this point—total rejection by his own people, the implacable opposition of the religious leaders, the failure of his disciples, his crucifixion and death. It is just as well we don't know everything in advance as we set out on a particular course in life, embrace a particular vocation, or choose a life's partner. Indeed, if we knew all that would transpire we might be tempted not to start out at all, and our lives, both ours and that of others, would be poorer.

So we pray trusting in God's help, step onto the stage, and the curtain goes up. It's showtime. And we hear a voice from the wings, from an actor who has already played the part preeminently well, saying, "Break a leg."

MONDAY OF THE
FIRST WEEK

Loving the Sinner

"You shall love your neighbor as yourself," it says in the book of Leviticus. Jesus agrees.

But what if you don't love yourself? Regrettably, with some of us that can be a real problem. There are those who are filled with self-hate and self-loathing. Their self-esteem is zero, and dropping. Now granted, there are things that we have said or done in our lives that we deeply regret and are very much ashamed of. Sometimes rightly so. Still, although one may appropriately hate the sin, one should not hate the sinner, even, perhaps especially, in one's own case; that is, if love of neighbor depends upon love of self.

It is possible to counter feelings of self-hate. One can say that God created all things good, ourselves included. "And God saw that it was good," is a common refrain at the end of each day of creation in the first chapter of Genesis. However, that may not help, since it means that if I was made good, but have not been good, then it's all my own fault. It may be true to say that God does not create junk; however, we are familiar with the possibility of thoroughly trashing a life.

Or one may say that God so loved the world that he sent his only begotten son to redeem the world, ourselves included. I must certainly be worth something if I am redeemed by the very Son of God. In other words, if Jesus died to save sinners, and even if I am the very worst, then I have been justified, made good in the sight of God through the blood of the Lamb. All my sins have been washed away. I am as clean as a shiny new penny.

One would think that this should solve the problem of self-hate. It would, if I didn't keep on sinning. It would, if I could somehow manage to make my conversion to the ways of righteousness stick. But, as we know, there is that ugly four-syllable word: *recidivism*. I seem to fall into the same old sins time and time again [and I really hate this image] like a dog returning to its vomit (Prov 26:11).

Or one could say that if I don't love myself, then I will be unable to love my neighbor as myself, as I am commanded by God to do. But that, of course, is precisely the problem: I don't love myself. But God loves me, one will say. No argument. But how and why he should do so, I do not understand. But he just does, and unconditionally. I don't understand that either.

We have hit a brick wall. We have run into a mystery, the mystery of divine love, a love for which there is no why.

Though there is that great old Protestant hymn that goes: "Jesus loves me, this I know, for the Bible tells me so...."

It all comes down to that: faith—"this I know"—belief in the revelation of God, faith in the revelation that is God's Son.

TUESDAY OF THE FIRST WEEK

Water into Wine

We are aware of the importance of water for life on earth.

Water was very much an issue in ancient Israel. Then, as now, Palestine was a region poor in water resources. Thus, wells had to be dug and cisterns hewn out of the rock to collect and retain the rainwater that fell during the winter months for the long hot dry summers. For a people that had wandered for years in the wilderness or on the steppes of the ancient Orient, even the scarce water resources of Palestine must have seemed like the proverbial Garden of Eden. Indeed, in Ezekiel (47:1 ff), the streams flowing from Jerusalem were seen as a harbinger of Paradise. The God of the Hebrews was recognized as the one who sent the needed rain to water the earth and make it fruitful.

Such is the background for the magnificent verses in chapter 55 of Isaiah that use the image of the rain and the snow coming down from heaven—and not returning back to the heavens (in evaporation) until they have watered the earth and made it fertile and fruitful—for the word of God itself. That word, going forth from the mouth of God, does not return empty, but accomplishes what it was sent out to do.

The word of God is, of course, the revealed word given to the chosen people in the law and the prophets. It is the law, the word of God given to Moses. But it is no less the words of the prophets sent to his people through the ages to call them to repentance. A common refrain in the prophetic books is "Thus says the Lord."

For Christians, the Word is also the Second Person of the Blessed Trinity, the Word made flesh that dwelt among us. That spoken Word come down from heaven does not return empty either, since it returns with all those immersed and cleansed in the waters of baptism and made fruitful in good works. As the rains falling on the vineyard make the grapes juicy and ready to be crushed, fermented, and aged into wine, so the creative Word of God brings forth the fine wine of mercy, compassion, and forgiveness.

I'll drink to that.

WEDNESDAY OF THE FIRST WEEK

Failure

"Nineveh," says the book of Jonah, "was an enormously large city; it took three days to go through it" (3:3).

Well, I can imagine someone saying the same thing about Los Angeles or some other megacity in today's world. In fact, I can readily believe that backpacking from one end of Los Angeles to the other might indeed take three days.

There is something about large cities. They are big and, in the view of people from small towns or from the country, they are wicked. The psalmist says that sin and troubles are within its walls, its streets never free from oppression and fraud (Ps 55:10–12). Maybe that's why those from the countryside like to go to the big wicked city—it's much more interesting, it seems, than life in the small town.

The people of Nineveh repented with the preaching of Jonah. And they were Gentiles. The generation to whom Jesus preached did not repent. And these were the chosen people, those to whom, time and time again, God had sent his prophets. That is why Jesus says that the citizens of Nineveh would rise up with the current generation and condemn it for "see, something greater than Jonah is here!" (Lk 11:32).

It was a supreme disappointment to Jesus that his own people did not respond to his teaching about the reign of God. Just as it was a disappointment to Paul, also a Jew, that the chosen people did not respond to his preaching regarding the

Messiah, the Christ crucified. Rejection by one's own is always the hardest. The crowds pressed around Jesus, listening to his words with pleasure. But the religious leaders of the people remained totally unmoved, as they had been unmoved by the preaching of John the Baptizer. And they would turn the crowds against Jesus.

Failure and rejection is never easy. However, if Jesus is our guide, and we are his followers, we can expect failure. The parent who sees a beloved child take a wrong direction in life, cease the practice of his or her faith, may ask in anguish, "Where did I fail?" It is likely to be the wrong question, and only promotes useless feelings of guilt. Nothing in the gospels indicates that Jesus ever asked this question of himself. He was certainly saddened by the rejection of himself and of his message. But the sadness was for those who had rejected him because they were his people.

Anyone who thinks that disappointment is not a part of life has not lived very long. However, anyone who thinks that it is not possible to get beyond seeming, or real, failure has not really understood life in the light of Jesus' gospel and the resurrection.

THURSDAY OF THE FIRST WEEK

When to Pray

Queen Esther was in trouble. She was between a rock and a hard place. If she went into the king's presence unbidden, she was taking her life in her hands. If she did not go into the king's presence and plead with him for herself and for her people, she, and they, were certain to perish at the hands of their enemies.

She was in trouble indeed. So she prayed. Which is what we should do if we are in trouble, have troubles, or are troubled.

Troubles is a plural word, because troubles come in bunches—not necessarily one after another, but sometimes all at the same time. Nicholas Steno, a scientist and philosopher from the seventeenth century, says that calamities always come in threes.

We pray not only when we are in trouble, in situations we have difficulty finding our way out of, or when things weigh us down, even overwhelm us; we also pray when we are troubled, anxious about we know not precisely what—the feeling that all is not well or soon will not be. Or we can be all too aware of what it is that troubles us, and we experience fear, or even panic.

When I am troubled thus, anxious about what may be out there in the dark, I utter a prayer learned as a child, which still serves me in good stead: "Angel of God, my guardian dear, to whom God's love commits me here, ever this day be at my side to light, to guard, to rule, and guide. Amen."

When the troubles come in bunches, I tell the Lord that it is all too much. I just don't know where to start getting things to come out right. My world appears to be coming down about my ears and I am at a total loss how to deal with it; everything is just too complicated and is simply beyond me and my abilities. I need help, serious help.

I realize that I am asking God to be a sort of executive secretary. However, he generally obliges anyway. Of course, the troubles may not be my own but those of someone near and dear to me, someone I am entirely powerless to help. I pray then, too.

Indeed, we should not simply pray when we, or others, are in trouble, have troubles, or are troubled. We should also praise God just for who and what he is. And we should periodically thank God for the scrapes he has gotten us out of, or the batch of troubles that he made disappear before they ever got to us.

FRIDAY OF THE FIRST WEEK

The Tongue

James is, of course, correct. In chapter three of the letter of James, it says that the tongue may be a small member of the body, but a most powerful one. It can be used for good, praising God, and it can be used for ill, cursing a brother or sister made in the image and likeness of God. James goes on to say that while wild animals have been tamed by humans, no one has yet managed to tame the human tongue, a restless evil, full of deadly poison.

We are certainly aware of the power of language and of speech. One may note that the Latin *lingua* is the word for both the tongue and for language. There is power in words, in language, as there is in the tongue by which those words are uttered. An orator, a lawyer, or a commercial on television can succeed in persuading us of something which is not true. The law is very much aware of the power of language. There are laws against libelous statements. The freedom of speech may be a right according to the Constitution; it is not, however, an absolute one. In recent times, we are more sensitive to "politically incorrect" speech.

We sometimes forget, though, that silence is also a part of language. There is the silence that enables us to distinguish between words in the flow of speech. There is the pregnant pause used by the actor to let the words or action of the drama sink in. Timing is crucial to the art of the comedian. But there is also the silence of the "silent treatment," which can be more cruel than outright words. There are relatives, family members, coworkers, or confreres who have not spoken to each other for years. Organizations, enterprises, families can self-destruct from the lack of communication.

In today's gospel, Jesus comes down hard against words spoken in anger, against abusive speech, so much so that if someone has anything against us, we are to leave our gift at the altar and first go to be reconciled with that person.

The gift on the altar is meant to reconcile the one who is offering the gift with God. And important as that is, Jesus insists that reconciling with one's brother or sister must come first.

The simple but sincerely meant words, "I'm sorry," are among of the most powerful words in any language.

SATURDAY OF THE FIRST WEEK

Being Perfect

Recently I got into an e-mail argument with a former fellow student over the issue of ethics. He insisted that we have a moral obligation to do the greater of two goods. I argued, instead, that we have no more than a moral obligation to do the lesser of two evils.

However, I granted that a religious ethic might prescribe not only the greater of two goods but even more than that, as Jesus does in the closing sentence of today's gospel: "Be perfect, therefore, as your heavenly Father is perfect" (Mt 5:48). Now *that* is heavy-duty morality.

One's first response to such a demand might understandably be "Give me a break. I'm having enough trouble being a decent human being, let alone being a perfectly divine one."

But Jesus insists: "Be perfect, therefore, as your heavenly Father is perfect." The demand seems exorbitant, literally out of this world. Which it is. So how can Jesus insist upon it?

Well, in what does divine perfection consist? It is contained in a couple of Hebrew words that are used throughout the Bible, especially in the Psalms, to characterize the nature of God: *hesed* and *emeth*. *Hesed* means kindness, mercy, love, compassion; *emeth* means fidelity, trustworthiness. The two taken together mean keeping the covenant relationship of love faithfully. This is the perfection that Jesus demands of his disciples. It means showing mercy and compassion, faithfully and with constancy, toward our brothers and sisters in the same way that our heavenly Father, faithfully and with constancy, shows loving and compassionate mercy toward us.

However, Jesus reminds us that the brothers and sisters to whom we are to show mercy and compassion may also be our enemy. However, unlovable as a particular person may be in our eyes, we must always remember that God finds something in him or her to love—"although God knows *what!*" we may think—and therefore we must do the same.

After all, we are to be perfect just as our heavenly Father is perfect.

SECOND SUNDAY OF LENT

Transfiguration

"And he was transfigured before them, and his clothes became dazzling white, such as no one on earth could bleach them," says the Gospel of Mark (9:2–3). There was also a vision of Moses and Elijah, and a voice from the clouds, "This is my Son, the beloved. Listen to him." Then they came down from the mountain.

In our lives transfiguration events seem few and far between. More often, there is not light, but darkness, a feeling of failure, the sadness of a loss, a grieving process that must simply be gone through. We do not feel the presence of Jesus, but rather his absence from our cares and concerns, and from the burdens we are forced to bear.

Our feelings, real as they may seem to us, are not perhaps the best gauge of reality. The Jesus that transfigured himself on the mountain is the same Jesus that walked down the mountain with the disciples in his fully human nature, one like our own, a human nature that knows what we feel and how we feel, and can fully sympathize with our trials and burdens. For Jesus also experienced darkness, the feeling of failure, and the sadness of seeing a disciple, before whom he had been transfigured, deny three times that he even knew him.

Through all this Jesus remained God's beloved, and we, even in the midst of our difficulties, must remind ourselves that we also remain Jesus' beloved brothers and sisters, the Father's beloved sons and daughters.

In this life, transfigurations don't happen every day. Still, the Jesus that was transfigured on the mountain is the same Jesus that walks along with us as we make our journey through life.

MONDAY OF THE SECOND WEEK

Measures

"What goes around comes around," we say. Or, as Jesus puts it, "The measure you give will be the measure you get" (Mt 7:2).

We are familiar with the phenomenon of children who treat their parents shabbily, not only failing to return their generous love, but even making the task of parenting more difficult. And it is not unusual for the pattern to repeat itself in the next generation, with their children causing them as much grief as they caused their own parents. The sins of the parents are visited upon their offspring, and these, in turn, come back to haunt their offspring when they become parents. The prophet Jeremiah quotes an adage from his day: "The parents have eaten sour grapes, and the children's teeth are set on edge" (Jer 31:29). However, both Jesus and Jeremiah say that it doesn't have to be that way.

Within the last few years we have become all too aware of the phenomenon of child sexual abuse, not only in society but even more scandalously in the church. It is particularly dreadful since the persons who abuse the young are in positions of trust, and this means that not only is the child abused, but their trust is abused as well. What makes such abuse especially heinous is that those who are abused suffer life-long psychological damage and, more often than not, grow up to be child abusers themselves.

Again, Jesus and Jeremiah say that it doesn't have to be that way. The cycle can be, indeed must be, broken. And Jeremiah indicates how it can be when he says: "But all shall die for their own sins; the teeth of everyone who eats sour grapes shall be set on edge" (Jer 31:30). In other words, the individual must be held responsible for what he or she has done, and dealt with in such a way that the vicious cycle does not get repeated but is forever broken.

But you may ask, does not Jesus in his teaching preach forgiveness, being compassionate, not judging or condemning, so that we will be forgiven, not be judged and condemned? Indeed. But he is also saying what Matthew says, "The measure you give will be the measure you get." Those who insist upon eating sour grapes must expect that their teeth will be set on edge, that they will be held accountable for what is their own doing.

TUESDAY OF THE SECOND WEEK

Teachers

Everyone is, of course, a teacher. Parents are the first, and the most important, teachers. The language we first speak is learned at our mother's knee. And, as we know, teaching and learning are not confined to the classroom. Young persons learn as much from their peers—whether for good or for ill—as they learn from their teachers in school.

However, what we are taught and what we learn are not necessarily the same thing. There is often a slip between the cup and the lip. Many a teacher reading a student's exam may utter an exasperated, "I didn't say that." I recall teaching catechism many years ago, and asking one of the seventh graders to name the evangelists. The answer: "Matthew, Martin Luther, and John."

Jesus says that we are to call no one our teacher, and avoid being called teacher. There is only one teacher, the Messiah, the anointed one. Indeed, teachers teach truths, passing on what is known to the next generation. The Messiah, on the other hand, taught the Truth, with a capital "T." And what did the Teacher—also with a capital "T"—teach? He taught that God is love. And the Messiah can teach this as the Truth, since he is the very Word of God made flesh out of love for sinful humanity: "God so loved the world that he sent his only son…" (Jn 3:16). There is only one Teacher teaching this Truth, the Truth that he himself is. That is why "…you have one instructor, the Messiah" (Mt 23:10).

Many of the teachers we are familiar with teach a particular subject: mathematics, literature, a language, science. They attempt to teach the student how to think like a mathematician, a chemist, a physician, a lawyer. They hope to teach the student how to be a teacher, that is, how to teach themselves, how to learn on their own, how to be self-starters.

The divine Teacher can teach the disciples, the learners, to learn on their own, to become self-starters, and thus themselves become teachers with the aid of divine grace. And only the divine Teacher can do this—make the disciple like the Teacher. As it says in the Gospel of Luke (6:40), "A disciple is not above the teacher, but everyone who is fully qualified will be like the teacher."

WEDNESDAY OF THE SECOND WEEK

Service

The mother of James and John was a good Jewish mother. She wanted her sons to succeed, to have the top positions in the organization. And she was willing to push their cause if need be, however gently, or even not so gently. After all, she knew they were good boys, and Jesus was getting a first-class deal in getting her two fine sons. They deserved, in return, to be at the top.

Of course, if we have read ahead in the Gospel of Matthew, we know that the positions at the right and left hand of the suffering Messiah are already taken. They are taken by the two thieves who are crucified on either side of him (Mt 27:38).

Jesus points to the downside of having a position of authority in his kingdom—drinking the cup of suffering that he is to drink. He also points to the meaning of that authority in his organization. It is not one of lording it over others, throwing your weight around, flaunting your power. That is what the rulers of the nations do. Exercising authority in Jesus' kingdom means service; and the one "at the top" is to serve the needs of all. Pope St. Gregory the Great referred to himself as the *servus servorum Dei*, the servant of the servants of God. In the history of the church, this is true of many popes. On the other hand, some popes, reigning gloriously, looked more like secular potentates.

One area in which those in authority must be extremely careful is relative to prophetic voices in the church. In First Thessalonians (5:19ff), St. Paul says, "Do not quench the Spirit.

Do not despise the words of prophets." Test those words, indeed. And there is a way of testing them: "You will know them by their fruits" (Mt 7:16a). These fruits are not simply the effect the words have but also the actions of the prophet. Those in authority need to exercise *discretio spirituum*, be good judges of character, and be able to discern a spirit that upbuilds the church from one that does not. Hence, the spirits that point to something amiss in the church should not be squelched or persecuted, even though their message may be annoying and uncomfortable. Those who went after Jeremiah were not doing Judah or Jerusalem any good.

In chapter 61 of the *Rule of Benedict*, the author notes that the abbot should prudently listen to the stranger monk visiting the monastery who in all humility makes some criticisms or observations, "since he may have been sent by God for precisely that purpose."

The critic, the prophet, the whistle-blower may be a first-class pain in the neck. Still, organizations, communities, and the church, need them. They can perform an invaluable service to those whose obligation it is to serve the needs of all.

THURSDAY OF THE SECOND WEEK

Ghosts

There are ghost stories about monasteries. One I have heard in many a monastery has to do with a novice, unable to sleep, entering the darkened abbey church to pray. At one of the side altars, there is an unknown priest saying Mass. The novice assists at the Mass, after which the priest departs for the sacristy. The next morning he mentions the incident to the novice master, who asks the novice to describe the priest. "Hmmm, that sounds like Father Isadore. He died a couple of years ago." At which point the novice's jaw drops and the eyes grow wide. "He must have failed to say a Mass intention for which he took a stipend, and had to come back from Purgatory to satisfy the obligation."

I have no way of knowing whether such stories are true or not. But I have heard variations of essentially the same story in many different monasteries, and in different languages. The telling and retelling of such stories may be to encourage a scrupulous care in fulfilling Mass obligations, lest one be obliged to come back from Purgatory, offer Mass in a darkened church, and frighten the novices.

In the story in today's gospel about Lazarus and Dives, we have the makings of a good ghost story. But it doesn't happen. Jesus may not have been into ghost stories. Dives, consigned to hell at least in part because he egregiously ignored the needs of Lazarus, the beggar at his gate, fails to talk Abraham into sending Lazarus to relieve his sufferings. So he tries to talk Abraham into sending Lazarus to his father's house to warn—scare the hell out of—his five brothers so that they will not come to the horrible place in which Dives finds himself.

Jesus resists the temptation to tell what might have been a great ghost story, suggesting that for some people even coming back from the dead will not necessarily do the trick, that is, lead to a change of life and conversion. In his gospel, Luke reminds his readers that there are those who will not be convinced even if one, like Jesus, rises from the dead.

Be that as it may, priests should carefully fulfill their Mass obligations lest they be obliged to come back from Purgatory, say Masses in darkened churches, and frighten the novices.

FRIDAY OF THE SECOND WEEK

Cash Money

From a cursory look at today's readings, one may come to a conclusion that Jesus was worth more money than Joseph. After all, Joseph was sold by his brothers to the Ishmaelites for twenty pieces of silver, whereas Judas got thirty pieces of silver for betraying Jesus. Of course, no amount of money paid for Jesus, or Joseph, could be the measure of their worth.

On the one hand, there are exorbitant salaries garnered by sports figures, and on the other hand, relatively paltry sums paid to teachers. Of course, economists would remind us that it is always difficult to determine the value of a service. A haircut is a haircut, but the price may be decidedly different if it is Joe's Barbershop around the corner, or Giorgio's of Beverly Hills.

In today's story from the Gospel of Matthew, about the absentee landlord and the sharecroppers, the vineyard owner was only demanding what was his due, his share of the harvest. Not only did he not receive it, but his servants were insulted, mistreated, and killed by the tenant farmers.

The theme of Israel as the Lord's vineyard is a rich one in the Bible, and Jesus uses it effectively in this story. God had sent prophet after prophet to remind the Israelites of their side of the covenant relationship. Finally, he sent his son—"They will respect my son."

We know the story. The son was not only rejected, but dragged outside the vineyard, outside the walls of Jerusalem, and slain.

But that is not the end of the story.

It was not really about the money. It was never really about the money. After all, was the money the only issue with Judas? What was thirty pieces of silver? A month's wages. Could Judas not have bargained for more, given the authorities' desire to be rid of Jesus?

So, again, it was not really about the money. The story is about the mystery of evil. It is about the death of the Messiah, which all of a sudden clears up at least one aspect of the mystery of evil. Human failure, human sin, does not jeopardize God's plan of salvation. Also, God can always obtain, indeed create, new personnel to make that or any other plan work out the way he wants it to work out.

It may be hard to get good help. But not for God.

SATURDAY OF THE SECOND WEEK

Shoes

The son had hit the Jewish equivalent of the gutter. He was broke. He was starving. He even no longer had shoes for his feet. And worst of all, here he was, a Jew, having to take care of pigs! He had definitely hit rock bottom. He could not sink any lower.

Sometimes we have to hit rock bottom. We have to come to the realization that so far as extricating ourselves from an impossible situation, lifting ourselves up by our own bootstraps, it's simply not going to happen today, tomorrow, not ever. It's the gutter. And part of the nature of a gutter is that it is a rut, and we are flowing down it toward whatever the gutter drains into.

The young man finally "came to his senses," Luke says (15:17), literally "came to himself." He came to the conscious realization that life does not have to be this way, that the direction in which his life was flowing did not have to be down the drain. Even being a hired hand on his father's farm would be better than where he was. Granted, he would have to admit that he had made a mistake, a big mistake. But that would be obvious as soon as his father saw him. He did not even have shoes. He may be unable to change his life on his own, but his father could. So he would return to his father's house.

He is able to complete only part of his prepared speech before his father has ordered out the finest robe, a ring for his finger, and (thank God!) shoes for his earth-burned feet, and commanded a feast to celebrate his safe return.

During the feast, the young man may have wondered if it was all a dream from which he would soon awaken, especially when he sees his father leaving the feast to persuade his brother to join the celebration. But he does not awaken. This is real. This is forgiveness, being home again, the revival of a remembered love, gratitude for a father who never gave up on him, even if he had given up on himself.

So where does life go from here? Things are definitely on the up side. The gutter is behind him. The sewer is not the end of the story.

And he's got shoes.

THIRD SUNDAY OF LENT

Spring-Cleaning

About this time of year, when I was growing up, there was spring housecleaning. Of course, our mother did most of the work, but we had to help. Among the tasks were taking all the dishes and stuff out of the cupboards, removing the old butcher paper and putting down new, cleaning out the refrigerator and scrubbing the interior, dusting and polishing, taking down and washing the curtains, and (my job) cleaning the windows inside and out. This involved a bucket of hot water liberally laced with vinegar, a sponge, and a pile of old newspapers. To this day, whenever I smell vinegar I think of window cleaning. But there is one thing I never understood: how using old newspapers covered with black ink on both sides could get the windows clean. But they did.

In the Gospel of John (2:13–25), we find Jesus involved in a little spring-cleaning. He was cleansing the temple. There were activities going on there that he did not deem a proper part of worship in his father's house.

The religious authorities demanded of Jesus a sign authorizing him to do this. They missed the point. The cleansing of the temple was itself the sign. They just didn't like the sign.

Lent is a time for spring-cleaning in our lives, a time for getting rid of some of the clutter, dusting off and polishing some old virtues, such as patience and kindness, working on some pious practices, such as holy reading and almsgiving.

During the spring-cleaning process we came across the clothes we had outgrown or not worn in years. The clothes, and some of the other stuff, especially from the garage, were boxed to be given to the Goodwill. Lent is about prayer and fasting, but it is also about giving to the poor, to those who are in need.

The things we do during Lent may seem insignificant, and often they are, but they have real, if less than obvious, effects in our lives and in the lives of others.

MONDAY OF THE
THIRD WEEK

Following Directions

I hate reading directions. I always figure that I'm intelligent enough to figure it out for myself, whether it is putting something together from a kit or a new software program. And let's face it: some directions seem to be written for third graders by third graders.

Then something goes wrong. You miss a step, or do the steps in the wrong order, and you end up with an extra piece, or your finished product just doesn't look like the one on the box.

So you have go back and read the stupid directions. Then it is necessary to take apart what was put together, go back to where the step was missed, or completely start over. Of course, this takes more than twice the time it would have taken if you had read the directions to begin with. But I hate reading directions.

Naaman the Syrian didn't like following directions either. After all, he was a successful Syrian general, and didn't need to be told how things should be done. So would he follow the simple directions given by Elisha the prophet to bathe seven times in the Jordan to be cured of his leprosy? "Poof," said Naaman, "we've got better rivers than that in Damascus."

Fortunately, Naaman had servants who could remind him that what the prophet prescribed was not all that difficult and suggested, tactfully, that he should simply follow directions.

So he did, with a happy result.

What religion is about, as Cardinal Newman once remarked, is authority and obedience. It is heeding what is said by one who has our best interests, our growth, at heart. (The word *authority* comes from *augere,* which means to increase, make to grow.) Religion is also about following directions. And in the long run, as we know, following the directions saves a lot of time and eliminates mistakes. For if we don't get off on the wrong track, we don't have to go to all the time and trouble to get back on the right track.

It is always helpful to have people around us, genuine friends, who will remind us that we are off course. What we need is the humility to go back and read the directions.

TUESDAY OF THE THIRD WEEK

Forgiving Oneself

There are magic numbers. Some people who play the lottery have elaborate schemes for picking the "winning numbers." The spread in the score between winner and loser in the Super Bowl may determine how a trader invests in the stock market. For the ancient Pythagoreans the number ten *(deka)* was sort of a magic number. For the Hebrews, on the other hand, seven was a special number—the symbol of perfection.

So when Peter asks Jesus how many times he should forgive someone who wrongs him, perhaps that's why he felt safe asking, "Seven times?" Jesus would surely concur with perfection, with perfect and complete forgiveness of one's brother or sister. Peter's jaw must have dropped when Jesus significantly upped the ante from perfection to superperfection—"Not seven times, but, I tell you, seventy-seven times." In other words, human forgiveness is to imitate the unconditional forgiveness of God.

A tall order. Yet, Jesus forgave the people who rejected him and his teaching. He died for their salvation. He forgave the disciples who fled at the first sign of danger. After the resurrection he reestablished table fellowship with them. He forgave Peter for denying him. Not only did he retain him in the position of leadership among the apostles, he confirmed him in that role. And he forgave those who engineered his crucifixion. "Father, forgive them; for they do not know what they are doing" (Lk 23:34). To take what Jesus had to take from his enemies, and from his friends, required a seventy-times-seven-times brand of forgiveness.

But did Jesus forgive Judas, his betrayer? One can readily understand how much Judas's betrayal must have hurt. Here was one whom he had specifically chosen, one upon whom he had lavished his love, yet one who had betrayed him into the hands of his enemies—with a kiss! One of the ugliest things about the breakup of a marriage is the way the expartners can use the intimate knowledge they have of each other to say and do hurtful things.

So, did Jesus forgive his betrayer? Indeed. "Father, forgive them." The problem was that Judas could not forgive himself: "…and he went and hanged himself" (Mt 27:5).

In the same way that it is impossible to love another unless we love ourselves, so it is not possible to ask forgiveness of another if we are unable to forgive ourselves and admit that we were simply wrong.

WEDNESDAY OF THE THIRD WEEK

Jewish Christianity

Protestants like to think that Pauline Christianity triumphed over Petrine Christianity. However, in the record of the controversy over the extent to which Gentile Christians should observe the Mosaic Law, we have only Paul's side of the story: "If you, though a Jew," Paul says to Cephas, "live like a Gentile and not like a Jew, how can you compel the Gentiles to live like Jews?" (Gal 2:14). We get a glimpse of the truth, how the matter really resolved itself, in that strange mix that was worked out in Jerusalem, sometimes termed the first church council. The Gentiles were to abstain from things polluted by idols, fornication, whatever had been strangled, and from blood (Acts 15:20).

Catholics, on the other hand, like to think that Petrine Christianity won out. However, by the time Peter got to Rome there was already a well-established Christian community there, basically a Jewish Christian community, likely deriving from James, "the Lord's brother." Paul attempted to curry favor with this church in his letter to the Romans, but failed, as likely did Peter. The view that Christianity was anything other than a sect of Judaism would have upset the *modus vivendi* that Christians, Jewish Christians, had worked out with Rome.

This is, perhaps, the context within which to understand the words put on the lips of Jesus in the Gospel of Matthew: "Do not think I have come to abolish the law and the prophets; I have come not to abolish but to fulfill" (Mt 5:17). Indeed, the Jesus of the Gospel of Matthew goes to great pains to draw out the deeper meaning behind the precepts of the law.

Rome has always prided itself on the fact that no heretic ever came out of the Roman schools. Which is not quite true. There was Marcion, who died around AD 160. His emphasis upon the gospel of love, to the exclusion of the law, led him to jettison the whole of the Old Testament. Clearly this could not have sat well with the traditions of a Jewish Christianity.

And it could not sit well with Christianity, period! To sever the tree from its roots means the death of the tree. To imagine a Christianity without Judaism would be like trying to imagine what Christianity would be like had Jesus, and the apostles, not been Jews.

Indeed, the psalms remain the basic prayer book for Christians, just as it has always been the basic prayer book for Jews.

THURSDAY OF THE THIRD WEEK

Mules and Things

We hear what we want to hear. What we don't want to hear we simply don't hear. It is the all-too-common case of selective deafness.

In chapter seven, Jeremiah distinguishes between hearing and heeding. God speaks to his chosen people through the prophets. The message may register on their eardrums, but it goes no further; or it goes in one ear and out the other. At any rate, no heed is paid to the word that is spoken. They turn their backs on the one speaking; they harden their hearts, stiffen their necks. This isn't simply not listening, it is the stubborn refusal to take correction in any way, shape, or form, crossing their arms over their chest and daring anyone, God included, to convince them otherwise.

We know how difficult it is to correct others, because we know how difficult we find taking correction ourselves, even when it may be all too obvious that we are in need of it. We do not take correction from those we perceive as not really liking us. And we do not readily take correction from those who like us, since in their making the correction we may perceive such persons as among those who don't like us. In other words, we do not take correction from enemies because they are not our friends; and we do not take correction from our friends, since in correcting us they have, in a sense, become our enemies. In effect, correction becomes impossible. We are incorrigible.

However, God does have his ways. Like the owner of a stubborn mule who hits the animal over the head with a two-by-four in order to get its attention, God has ways of getting our attention. It may be a serious illness, the removal of something deeply treasured from our lives, a trial that tries our soul. We may ask: Why has God sent this illness, this trial, this sadness into my life? But we may need to ask deeper questions: Is God trying to tell me something, and I have not been listening? Is God attempting to turn me back around toward him?

FRIDAY OF THE THIRD WEEK

Good and Bad Company

In the Gospel of Mark, it is the chief priests and the scribes who are held responsible for the death of Jesus. The scribes were not merely those who knew how to read and write, who were able to draw up legal documents or petitions, write letters for those unable to write them, they were also experts in the law. They had to know the law to be able to write up such legal documents.

Given the large number of laws, there were discussions among the scribes, especially when it came to differences of opinion about which law was pertinent in a particular case, or about how to reduce the law to its essentials. So the scribe asks Jesus for his opinion on the question: Which is the first, the most basic, of the commandments?

One should not ascribe ill will to the scribe asking the question, as though he were merely trying to test or trap Jesus. Certainly, Jesus did not perceive it in that fashion. For when the scribe approves of Jesus' response, and expands further on the subject, Jesus says: "You are not far from the reign of God."

One can readily imagine that the scribe was not entirely comfortable with his sudden inclusion within Jesus' company. But there it was. He got more than he bargained for. But it was a good bargain, inclusion within a kingdom which, along with Jesus, was that of God. It is always good to be in good company.

Thus, one may hope that the scribe who asked the question did not join the bad company of those scribes who, along with the chief priests, pursued the death of Jesus. Those scribes had obviously failed to love their neighbor as themselves.

SATURDAY OF THE THIRD WEEK

Good Guys and Bad Guys

What is one to say about the Pharisee and the tax collector? The simple answer is to say that the Pharisee is proud and arrogant; the tax collector is humble and honest. End of sermon. But life and, above all, Jesus' parables are never so simple.

Let's begin with the tax collector. The tax collector in the parable is not one of the big fish. He is not one of the powerful publicans who obtained a franchise to collect taxes for a region of the Roman Empire, and then farmed out the actual collecting to the small fish like the tax collector in today's gospel. The tax collector in the gospel is, indeed, humble, his line of work humiliating. He was the hated local agent for an oppressive regime. Also, there was the taint of dishonesty attached to his profession. Finally, because they had frequent contact with gentiles at forbidden times, they tended to be ritually unclean. He's the bad guy in the story.

Now take the Pharisee. He was part of a lay reform movement in first-century Palestine. The Pharisee is the good guy in the story. But, you will say, he is a braggart, extols his own virtues, and is insufferably smug. However, is there anything wrong with his thanking God that he is not a thief, an adulterer, and the like, and that it is God who has enabled him to be a good person? Why shouldn't he toot his own horn? After all, he fasts not just once, but twice a week; and he is generous. He tithes. And does not St. Paul (in Phil 3:5–6) pride himself on being a good Pharisee and, as to righteousness under the law, blameless? Humility is truth. The Pharisee is not proud and arrogant but humble.

Jesus' parables have a way of turning things upside down. His hearers would have seen the Pharisee as the good guy and the tax collector as the bad guy. Yet, Jesus says that the tax collector leaves the temple justified, while the Pharisee does not. Wherein, then, lies the Pharisee's fault? What vitiates his otherwise proper prayer? It is contained in that one short phrase "…or even like this tax collector." The Pharisee thanks God that he has preserved him from being a thief, an adulterer, and so on—all well and good. He thanks God for preserving him from sin—but he adds "or even like this tax collector." Not only is the Pharisee judging, raising his eyebrows, and looking down his nose at the tax collector, but his standard of comparison is all wrong. He should not be comparing himself, his life, and obvious virtue with the poor tax collector, but with God. Recall Jesus' command: "Be perfect as your heavenly father is perfect." Thus, in spite of the Pharisee's virtues, there is at least one area in his life that needs genuine attention, namely, his disparaging attitude toward the poor tax collector.

FOURTH SUNDAY OF LENT

Artwork

The Romantics, since they were heavily into art, were sometimes wont to speak of the process of living as painting one's own portrait, as the attempt to paint the ideal self-portrait.

The difficulty with this view is that if we are the ones doing the portrait, it will most likely not be a great work of art. If we really want a masterpiece, then it is necessary to get a master artist to do it. For example, if a halo is to be painted about the head, then it will have to be put there by the divine painter. A human painter's attempt at this can only appear as hubris.

Painters who do portraits know where to begin. They often begin by sketching the eyes. If they can get the eyes right, the rest of the face, and the portrait, will take care of itself. The eyes are critical in human communication. When we converse with someone we look into their eyes. Experienced detectives insist that they can tell whether suspects are lying just by watching their eyes. In social interaction, eye contact is either sought or avoided, depending upon how one wishes to be related to. Lovers look deeply into each other's eyes, indeed feast on the vision.

Self-portraits are really a bad idea anyway. It implies taking a three-dimensional object (one's face) from a two-dimensional mirror-image and transferring it onto a two-dimensional canvas, while attempting to give it a three-dimensional feel. We are inherently suspicious of self-portraits, not only because of the mechanics involved, but also on account of the bias and prejudice of the one doing the portraying. The portraiture may not be one's ideal self, but a suspiciously idealized self.

The portrait we should want painted is the one that the master painter produces. For God knows how best to paint the portrait, having created not only the model but the canvas, and the context of the life that would be portrayed. As it says in the Letter to the Ephesians (2:10), we are God's handiwork, his work of art *(poeima)*. And God knows the ideal model to sit for that portrait. It is not ourselves but God's Son, the Lord Jesus.

In a sense, God also starts with the eyes. For it is with the eyes of faith that we would begin to see ourselves fashioned in the image and likeness of God, and refashioned in the image and likeness of his Son.

MONDAY OF THE FOURTH WEEK

A New Earth

If you watch the ten o'clock news on a regular basis you may be inclined to think that society is "going to hell in a hand basket." There are reports of murders, kidnappings, robberies, and so forth, as well as reports about the perpetrators of those crimes being sought, apprehended, tried, and convicted. All the news seems to be bad. This is one of the reasons I seldom watch the ten o'clock news. I prefer to watch the eight o'clock news in the morning. It's a new day, and the world looks a little better at the start of the day.

Similarly, prophets are not all doom and gloom. Not all the news is bad. Sometimes the news is not only good, but very good. In chapter 65 of the prophet Isaiah, for example, we read that God is about to create new heavens and a new earth. If we believe the cosmologists, new heavens are constantly being created. The new earth, however, is what we are really interested in.

In this new and, shall we say, heavenly city, the heavenly Jerusalem, the bad things of the past will no longer be remembered. In place of the sound of weeping and crying there will be rejoicing and gladness. Instead of a life that is shortened by disaster or tragedy, the inhabitants of the new Jerusalem will live to a ripe old age, like a hundred years. "They shall build houses and inhabit them; they shall plant vineyards and eat their fruit" (Is 65: 21).

We are talking about *shalom*. We are talking about Jerusalem, which means City of Peace, living up to its name. This peace is not simply the absence of war, but something eminently positive: complete well-being.

Of course, we may say, "All very nice; but it is not the real world. The real world is the ten o'clock news." Well, yes and no. Such actions as someone helping out a neighbor in need, a person performing an act of kindness, a friend supporting someone who is grieving, don't make the news. Yet, these are the people who bring peace and well-being and help create a new earth.

My personal view is that they make up the majority. The ten o'clock news gives the wrong spin to the earth.

TUESDAY OF THE FOURTH WEEK

Illness

For those who are ill, especially those whose illness has become long term, perhaps terminal, feelings of discouragement and depression are common. An illness that just seems to linger on and on, with no end in sight, can leave one quite depressed. Something as minor as the common cold, which we seem unable to shake, can weigh heavily upon our minds. And psychologists will point out that such feelings can have a negative effect upon bodily health and upon the body's own powers to restore itself to health. Indeed, physicians are familiar with patients who, in such a mind-set, just give up and lose the will to live.

The man at the sheep pool who had been sick for a long time had largely lost hope. Hence Jesus' question: "Do you really want to be healed?" It was a basic question.

Those who deal with persons addicted to chemical substances, for example, are familiar with the situation. If the person does not really want to be cured, does not want to seek counseling, or does not want to go into treatment—or, if he or she is not convinced of the benefit, indeed the absolute necessity, of kicking the habit, it is simply not going to happen.

Similarly, we are aware of the extremely important function performed by hospital chaplains, not simply for the benefit of the patient's spiritual life, but for their physical healing as well. Jesus tells the sick person who had been cured to give up his sins, lest something worse befall him. Our sins, above all a pattern of sin, can have a serious impact on our physical health. Anger or hatred, or bearing a deep-seated and long-nursed grudge against another person, will have an effect on our health. By the same token, unless the sin is forgiven, unless that spiritual block is removed from one's life, the physical process of healing cannot begin.

We are not only body, but spirit also. Illness is not simply a question of physical disease or disability; the spiritual side of the human being is also intimately involved in our illnesses, and it may be necessary to address the spiritual issues in our life if the physical ones are to be taken care of.

WEDNESDAY OF THE FOURTH WEEK

Slavery

The economies of the ancient world were built upon slavery. This may not be surprising when it comes to the Romans who, throughout their history, were noted for a certain efficient, if sometimes brutal, practicality. However, we might wish that it had been otherwise with the Greeks, whose intellectual and scientific attainments we respect and admire.

One of the advances made by St. Benedict at the end of the Roman Empire was that of dignifying, even ennobling, human labor. Prior to Benedict all labor was servile, work done by slaves, something unworthy of a citizen. On the other hand, in chapter 48 of his Rule, "On the Daily Manual Labor," Benedict orders that there should be specified periods of manual labor, "for then are they truly monks if they live by the labor of their hands."

Jesus, of course, worked. He was the son of a carpenter. Paul worked at the trade of tentmaker. But God also worked, in the beginning creating the heavens and the earth (Gen 1:1). In the Gospel of John (5:17), Jesus says, "My Father is still working, and I also am working." What Jesus is working at is no longer the trade of carpenter, but a far more important task, a work that he sees his Father doing. It is creative work, the work of redemption, the salvific work of healing, of raising the dead to life, of freeing the prisoners from the darkness of prison and bringing them out into the light, as it says in the prophecy of Isaiah.

There are life situations in which we may feel trapped, imprisoned. It may be a degenerative disease, an abusive relationship, a job that is barely tolerable, or a joyless life. Like the slave in the ancient world, it may seem that the only escape is death.

However, there is not only the labor and work that we perform, there is also the work and labor that the Lord performs in us, the liberating and freeing labor that makes of us a new creation. Paul recognized slavery as a fact of life in his world, but he also indicated the way in which Christians can come to terms with whatever hopeless situation they encounter in life. As he says, "For whoever was called in the Lord as a slave is a freed person belonging to the Lord..." (1 Cor 7:22).

The only slavery that is total entrapment is slavery to sin. And from this we have been freed by the Lord Jesus.

THURSDAY OF THE FOURTH WEEK

Testimony

Actions speak louder than words. That is what Jesus says to those who do not listen to his words. He admonishes us to look at the works the Father has given him to accomplish. "These," says Jesus, "testify on my behalf that the Father has sent me."

There are prophetic gestures which speak louder than words. Jeremiah was famous for them. There was the time Jeremiah was commanded by God to bury his loincloth, dig it up, and exhibit the rotten garment to the people to show Israel's unfaithfulness to the covenant (chapter 13). There was the time Jeremiah walked around the city with a yoke on his neck to signify subjection to Babylon (chapter 27). And there was the time Ezekiel dug a hole in the city walls of Jerusalem and passed through it carrying his belongings to symbolize deportation from the city that he had pronounced doomed (chapter 12).

Jesus performed prophetic gestures as well, most notably driving the money changers out of the temple. But his most important gesture was being fixed to a cross set between heaven and earth. This action, his passion and death, spoke volumes. What it bespoke was the love of the Father toward sinful humanity.

Our lives are gestures. The work we do, the simple tasks of daily living that we perform—no matter how simple, prosaic, or humdrum they may appear to us—are important for us and for our salvation. They are our work, our task. We work out this our salvation in fear and trembling, as St. Paul says in Philippians 2:12.

We don't have to say anything. Sometimes there is little to be said, as there is little choice in the tasks we are called upon daily to perform.

At times we may have the impression that our lives are without meaning. However, that is not true. The life of each of us has the meaning that God gives it—his meaning, the meaning given by his cross and resurrection, the meaning that is his love—the only meaning that really matters.

FRIDAY OF THE FOURTH WEEK

Blessed Event

There is a theory in pediatrics that the fetus decides when it is going to come out. And what determines the time for the blessed event, the baby's exit from the womb, is when it senses that it is beautiful, and hence will be lovable and cuddly for its parents and all the relatives and friends of the family, who will gush, "What a beautiful baby!" or "Isn't she as cute as a bug's ear?" (Though I am really quite uncertain if a bug's ear is cute or not.)

As it says in the Gospel of John, even though there were those who wanted to arrest Jesus forthwith, they did not do so, "for his hour had not yet come."

What Jesus' enemies have in mind for him is not beautiful. As outlined in the passage from the Book of Wisdom (2:12–22), likely dating from the century prior to Jesus' death, what they have in mind is reviling him and torturing him, putting the just and innocent one to the test, trying his patience to see proof of his gentleness and, in the end, putting him to a shameful death.

There is nothing particularly beautiful about any of this. Certainly not for the one who will appear as a "man of sorrows," one struck down and afflicted, led like a lamb to the slaughter, to be cut off from the land of the living (Is 53).

Although not a beautiful picture from a worldly point of view, in terms of our salvation the matter is very much otherwise. For he was wounded for our transgressions, punished that we might be made whole, bruised that we might be healed. His life was an offering for our sin, making many righteous through his sufferings.

What it all meant was our rebirth into the kingdom of God so that we might come forth, reborn in the spirit, made manifest in all our beauty.

Through the death of the anointed one we are the blessed event.

SATURDAY OF THE
FOURTH WEEK

Resurrection

Jesus raised his friend Lazarus from the dead. However, Lazarus would have to die again.

Wasn't dying once bad enough? Well, not according to those who have had what are termed near-death experiences. As a result of the experience, such persons no longer have a fear of death, at least according to a hospital chaplain friend of mine who has collected some 150 such stories.

However, it should be pointed out that these are near-death *experiences*. They are *not* the real thing. One's actual death cannot be experienced, since with death all experience ceases, as the ancient Greek philosopher Epicurus noted, "When [death] is, we aren't."

Martha believes in the resurrection on the last day. Gradually, the notion of the resurrection had made its way into the religious thinking of Israel. Still, there were segments of people in the Jewish society in Jesus' time who did not believe in the resurrection, for example the Sadducees, as is evidenced in Mark's Gospel (12:18 ff). Jesus' response to them is that they understand neither the scriptures nor the power of God. Since the Sadducees believe only in the Pentateuch, the first five books of the Bible, Jesus quotes the Torah back to them: to whit, that God is the God of the living, the God of Abraham, Isaac, and Jacob, not the God of the dead. Further, he says they do not understand the power of the God, who, able to create life, is therefore also able to recreate a new and eternal life in one who has died.

What that life will be like we do not know. Nevertheless, we have the words of Paul in First Corinthians (2:9): "What no eye has seen, nor ear heard, nor the human heart conceived, what God has prepared for those who love him."

Dying is a matter of trust, not a trust in the miracles of medical science to restore us to life and health, much less keeping the body alive in its final stages, a life which may not really be worth living, but rather a trust in the power of God to raise us to eternal life in him.

FIFTH SUNDAY OF LENT

Life and Death, Death and Life

I don't particularly like telling this story. When I was young, the assistant priest in our parish took me and a companion up into the belfry of the church where the bells were hung. The tower was filled with small birds flying to and fro. The priest had quick hands, caught one of the birds, and gave it to me. I held it in my hand as I walked home. When it tried to escape I held it tighter. Just before reaching home the bird made one final desperate effort, pushing its feet against my hand. I squeezed tighter still. The head drooped to one side. I had killed it.

We know parents who hold onto their children this way, wanting them to remain at a certain age, being overprotective, not letting them grow and go free. The possessiveness of the parent holding on so tightly can be totally suffocating for the child or adolescent, to the point where he or she is unable to develop into a mature adult.

Regrettably, we can do the same thing to ourselves. Jesus said that the one who loves his life loses it. It is possible for us to hang on so tightly to the life we currently have, hanging on desperately to what we are at the moment, that we become incapable of moving or changing. We are in serious danger of losing everything. The refusal to change, remaining totally wrapped up in the self that we are, refusing to become the self that we are meant to become, a new and different self to which God may be calling us, is the surest way to be fettered to a self or a "world" that is doomed to self-destruct.

The rock climber who hangs on for dear life to where he or she is on the rock face will not make it to the top, and indeed may not make it back to the bottom either, stuck, and in a hopeless panic.

To refuse to grow and change when life, when God, indicates the direction of growth and change, is not the way to life but to its loss. On the other hand, accepting the death of a life that really ought to perish and accepting the life of love and service proffered by Jesus is to open up your life to its fullest potential.

The grain of wheat that does not fall into the earth and die remains but a grain of wheat. Planted in the soil, and dying, the grain becomes a seed productive of eternal life.

MONDAY OF THE
FIFTH WEEK

The Dead Weight of Sin

There is a nice touch in the story in chapter eight of John's Gospel about the woman caught in adultery. After Jesus has challenged those who would stone her to death by saying that only those without sin should cast the first stone, the evangelist notes that the audience began to drift away, one by one, beginning with the eldest. As one grows older, one accumulates more sins.

This is true not only of individuals but of nations, institutions, and organizations as well. From a religious point of view, empires fall not primarily because they are defeated in war or due to economic meltdown, but from internal rot. They decline and fall, crushed under the accumulated dead weight of their own sins: unwarranted aggression, greed, cruelty. The same, one would have to admit, is true of churches and religions as well.

If that is the case, then what of the Catholic Church, which has been around for millennia? Should not the church, for its sins, have disappeared centuries ago? Indeed, if one reads the history of the church, one would have to admit that on several occasions it came close to self-destructing. Yet, it did not. Well, did not Jesus promise that the gates of hell (death) would not prevail against it (Mt 16:18)? Indeed. However, the portals of death into which the church has, at times, haplessly wandered did not come only from without but, again, from within, like the internal rot of an evil empire.

Nonetheless, we believe in a church that is one, holy, catholic, and apostolic. And rightly so. This holiness does not mean that everything the members of the church, or its leaders, have done always was, or is, good, right, and proper. One would have to be more than naïve to believe that. Yet, unlike the individuals, the kingdoms, the empires of this world with their accumulated sins, the church, the bride of Christ, is ever new and ever renews herself. The church is always able to start over, revive its life in the Spirit, through the Spirit, repent and have its heart re-formed. This is not the bride of Christ receiving a periodic face-lift, tummy tuck, or plastic surgery to make an aging body look young again. No, renewal in the spirit works from the inside out, which is the only way renewed life can be effective in individuals, or in nations as well.

TUESDAY OF THE
FIFTH WEEK

Mystery

Reading the Gospel of John, especially chapters seven and eight, one would conclude that the crowds find Jesus to be one huge insoluble puzzle. They are split between those who regard him as the Messiah or as the Prophet who would announce the Messiah's appearance. And they are not in agreement regarding his origin, whether he is from Bethlehem, David's city, or from Galilee.

There is no puzzlement or lack of certainty on the part of the religious authorities: he is not the Messiah, nor is he the Prophet. The Prophet does not come from Galilee. And that's that.

The problem with certainty is that you can be certainly wrong, above all if your mind is made up beforehand. And when Nicodemus even suggests that it would be well to check out the facts, or hear what Jesus might have to say in his defense before being condemned, he is simply shouted down.

The crowd, nonetheless, remains puzzled, unsure not only about Jesus' identity but also about his origins. Jesus' answer to their concerns is to make his identity dependent upon his origins. He is neither from David's city nor from Galilee, but from the truthful One who sent him.

So when the crowd asks, "Well, then, who are you?" his answer is: "I am the one sent by the one who sent me." This is not very helpful. For what Jesus is saying, in effect, is that he is a mystery. In the technical theological sense, a mystery is something that cannot be understood before it is revealed, or fully understood even after it is revealed. In other words, a revealed mystery is still a mystery. Mysteries are catch-22 situations. If you insist upon understanding the mystery before you will believe, then you will never believe. On the other hand, if you must first believe the mystery before you will understand it, you will still not understand it. For it is a mystery.

Indeed, that is all you can do in the face of a mystery: believe. And some, John notes at the end of the gospel passage (Jn 8:30), came to believe in him because he spoke in this way.

He termed himself a mystery, but a life-giving and truthful one.

WEDNESDAY OF THE FIFTH WEEK

Sin and Sinner

King Nebuchadnezzar had a temper. When Shadrach, Meshach, and Abednego refused to worship the golden statue the king had set up, he became livid with rage at them. So he ordered the fiery furnace to be heated seven times hotter than usual and then had Shadrach, Meshach, and Abednego thrown into the white-hot flames. King Nebuchadnezzar was really mad.

In the Bible, we read of the wrath of God, that God becomes angry. And it will not do to say, after the manner of the heretic Marcion (who died about the year 160), that this is just the God of the Old Testament, whereas the God of the New Testament is a God of love. All we need do is read Paul's Letter to the Romans or the Book of Revelation to discover that the wrath of God is alive and well in the New Testament as well.

Nevertheless, there are some decided differences between God's anger and that of King Nebuchadnezzar. In the first place, although God may become angry he does not become livid with rage. The Lord of the universe does not lose his cool. Secondly, what makes God really angry is sin. He finds it personally distressing since it is, above all, hurtful to others. However, he is more understanding when it comes to the sinner.

Now it is perfectly true that if all people who suffer from headaches are guillotined there will be no more headaches. Similarly, if you get rid of all sinners you get rid of sin. But then who do you have left? God apparently tried this approach with the flood, and later concluded that it was a bad idea: "...and the waters shall never again become a flood to destroy all flesh" (Gen 9:15).

In Christ Jesus, on the other hand, God tried a different approach: get rid of the sin by having Christ die to destroy the power of sin in the lives of human beings, but save the sinner, so that the sinner is no longer a slave to sin. Thus, as it says in the Gospel of John (8:36), "So if the Son makes you free, you will be free indeed."

THURSDAY OF THE
FIFTH WEEK

War and Peace

Three religions, Judaism, Christianity, and Islam, all claim
Abraham as their father. Well, Christians claim him only as their
father in faith. Abraham believed God and his promise: the
promise of a son and descendents as numerous as the sands on
the seashore, and also the promise of a land, Canaan. God prom-
ised that from Abraham's loins would spring a host of nations.
And God said that he would give Abraham and his descendents
a land—Palestine—as their possession forever. One would have
to say that the children of Abraham in the flesh, and sometimes
those in the spirit, have been fighting over that land, and with
each other, ever since.

What is there about religion that causes wars? Of course, the
Buddhists maintain that it is because of the Christian, Jewish,
and Muslim belief in a personal God. Although *ahimsa*, nonvio-
lence, may be a tenet of the religions of Southeast Asia, it does not
always work out that way in real life.

Probably the question "What is there about religion that
causes war?" is the wrong question. Indeed, one might argue that
it is not the religions that cause war but their failure. *Jihad* in the
Muslim faith may be interpreted not as violence against unbe-
lievers, or even as the defense of Islam from external attack, but
rather as the war declared on the evil passions and desires within
the person, the hate and the anger that lead to physical violence
and war. In other words, it is just the opposite of the reading

given it by Islamic fundamentalists. The so-called "holy war" is the personal struggle involved in becoming holy.

Wars do not come out of religion, but from its lack. They do not come from God, no matter the extent to which his auspices are invoked, but from people's screwy and confused ideas of God. It is true that one of the titles of God in the Old Testament is *El Shaddai*, the Lord of Hosts. However, this is not the Lord of earthly might, but the Lord of the heavenly host. God's real army is not an army of steel and weapons, but of spirit and compassion. Earthly armies only kill and destroy, leaving devastation, mourning, and more hate in their wake. God's army favors the opposite: life and peace.

FRIDAY OF THE FIFTH WEEK

Blasphemy

In the Gospel of John, we are presented with a Jesus of profound theological depth. He is a figure who says: "I am the way, and the truth, and the life" (Jn 14:6). The Jesus of John's Gospel does not say: I am *a* way, *a* truth, *a* life, as though there were others. Rather, he says: I am *the* way, *the* truth, *the* life—there are no others. Jesus is saying: It's *my* way or no way; it's *my* life or no life—at least no *eternal* life. There are really no compromises possible here.

Eventually, in John's Gospel Jesus drops all the articles and nouns, and simply asserts: "I am." His listeners get the message, and immediately accuse him of blasphemy. And from the Jewish perspective, rightly so.

In chapter three of Exodus, Moses knows good and well that if he appears before the people of Israel with the message that the God of their ancestors has sent him to them, and they ask for his name, he had better come up with a good response. So he asks the burning bush for its name. And the voice from the bush that burns but is not consumed tells Moses to say to the Israelites: "I AM has sent me to you" (Ex 3:14).

So when Jesus drops all the predicates, the articles, and nouns, what is left with the subject "I" is only the bare verb "am," and the Jews immediately accuse him of blasphemy. Blasphemy is saying something bad, something really bad, something profoundly disrespectful, about the deity. In this context, at least so far as his Jewish listeners are concerned, it refers to Jesus' taking on divine prerogatives. It is bad enough that Jesus should claim to be the Messiah—and in no way did he look like any kind of Messiah they were even vaguely interested in—making himself equal to God was beyond the pale.

So they picked up stones to stone him to death.

Politics, the art of the possible, involves compromise. Jesus and his listeners had reached a point beyond which compromise of any sort had become possible.

SATURDAY OF THE FIFTH WEEK

One for All

Caiaphas is what ethical theorists would term a utilitarian. The principle of his ethics is that of social utility, what is eminently useful for the society as a whole: the greatest good for the greatest number. Caiaphas said that it was better that one man die than for an entire nation to have to perish" (cf. Jn 18:14).

Of course, the problem with utilitarian ethical theory is that the greatest good for the greatest number may be the least good for the few, and not at all good for a particular individual, in this case Jesus. But while the ready willingness to sacrifice the individual for the collectivity may seem callous, utilitarians, and Caiaphas, do have a point: the commonweal, the well-being of the community as a whole, may often take precedence over the private interests of the particular individual.

There are, of course, those who argue against capital punishment. It is entirely true that if a judicial mistake is made in a capital case and the wrong person is apprehended, tried, convicted, sentenced, and executed, the error cannot later be rectified, as it can in the case of innocent persons who languish in prison for crimes they did not commit. In the final analysis, one can hardly be in favor of capital punishment. There has to be a better way. As a Christian, on the other hand, one can hardly be absolutely opposed to capital punishment. For if there had been no capital punishment in the Roman Empire in the time of Jesus, then Jesus would not have been put to death, dying on the cross in atonement for our sins.

After noting Caiaphas's prophecy, the author of the fourth gospel goes on to say that Jesus would indeed die for the nation. And not just for the Jewish nation, but for the whole dispersed children of God. In other words, defective as aspects of utilitarian theory may be, the application of the principle of the greatest good for the greatest number was certainly the case with the death of Jesus. We, as beneficiaries of that sacrifice of the individual for the collectivity, must surely testify to this.

PALM SUNDAY

King of the Jews

Palm Sunday features Jesus' triumphal entry into Jerusalem, palms ripped from the trees and waved in the breeze, cloaks strewn on the road over which the prophet from Galilee rode into the city on a donkey to the accompaniment of hosannas from the crowd. It was the sort of demonstration that would make the religious authorities in Jerusalem nervous, because they knew it made the Romans nervous. On major Jewish feasts, extra soldiers were posted in the city, above all on the high holy feast of Passover when religious Jews flocked to Jerusalem to celebrate the feast. But if it drew religious Jews to the city from far and wide, could the religious nuts be far behind?

To those in power, religious and otherwise, Jesus seemed to be one of these nuts.

Hence, the first question Pilate asks of Jesus in Mark's Gospel is: "Are you the king of the Jews?" The Romans, if nothing else, were good administrators. So Pilate got right to the point. Basically, what he was asking was "Are you trouble?" Jesus' answer was ambiguous: "So it is said." Pilate did not pick up on the nuance. Trouble he was; king of the Jews he was not. For later, when Pilate offers the crowd a choice between releasing Barabbas or Jesus, they opt for Barabbas rather than the one they had given the title "king of the Jews." Under that title Jesus is mocked by the soldiers; under that inscription he is crucified. He is also ridiculed by the religious authorities, the chief priests, and the scribes, who wangled his death: "Let the Messiah, the King of Israel, come down from the cross...."

Just another one.

Of course, there's trouble, and there is *trouble*. There is the trouble that upsets the public order, disturbs the peace. But there are also those—the prophets—who are troubling for the status quo because it desperately needs troubling. And while it is possible to get rid of the prophetic voice by getting rid of the prophet, doing away with the message by doing away with the messenger, the troubles endemic in the current state of affairs may not be so easily disposed of. The untroubled consciences will still need to be disturbed, the out-of-whack state of affairs will still need to be upset, or else something even worse will transpire.

Indeed, it would not be long before everything would be very different from what it had been before.

Jesus was not just another religious nut.

MONDAY OF HOLY WEEK

The Gesture

By any standard it was an extravagant gesture as Judas recognized: Mary broke a container of very expensive perfume, nearly a year's wages for an ordinary day laborer, and poured it over Jesus' feet!

Jesus knew that his time was approaching. When we are anxious about something, an impending crisis, one that we clearly see coming, we need to be able to share our cares and concerns, our worries and fears with those who are closest to us, hoping for some consolation, some sympathy, some understanding. Jesus had already tried it, indeed several times, with his intimate disciples, but as the gospels indicate again and again, they did not understand.

His friend Mary did. There is no indication that he confided to her his personal fears and anxiety. She just knew, in the way that a good friend, someone close to you, just knows that you are deeply troubled about something, even when the friend does not know precisely what it is.

Mary performs a beau geste, a beautiful gesture. One can readily imagine how deeply appreciative Jesus was of her thoughtfulness and the expression of her concern.

It is a lesson for each one of us. When we see someone, a friend, a spouse, a parent, or a child who is down, we need to think of some beau geste. The gesture need not be extraordinary, or as extravagant as that of Jesus' friend. Nevertheless, whatever way we can show that we are there for one another in times of sadness or need may make all the difference in the world.

TUESDAY OF HOLY WEEK

Dark Night

"And it was night," says the last sentence of verse 30 in chapter 13 of John's Gospel. It was night in more than one sense, as words and expressions are often understood in more than one sense in the Gospel of John. It was night because Satan had already entered into the heart of Judas. Judas had eaten the morsel of bread dipped in the dish, whereby Jesus had indicated to Peter the one who would betray him.

It was night not simply because of the darkness and its evil power in the heart of Judas, it was night also because it is in the dark that the deeds of darkness take place. Crimes are best bred in the dark; criminals prefer to work under cover of darkness.

It was a night into which Jesus also would enter to do combat with the powers of darkness. He would overcome those principalities and powers, the power of sin and evil that infest the darker side of human hearts. Jesus would become sin in order to overcome sin, evil, and death, the dark weapons of those principalities and powers. He would enter the darkness of death to overcome that final enemy.

In the events commemorated during Holy Week, we pass into the memory of a time when it was night, when everything went dark: "When it was noon, darkness came over the whole land until three in the afternoon" (Mk 15:33). The earth and sky went dark, overcast with a pall. And in recalling the events of Jesus' passion and death, we also enter into the darkness of that day, as into a dark tunnel. Though we do know how the story turns out—there is the light of the resurrection at the end of the tunnel. Still, if we are to enter into the remembered events of those days, we too must pass into the dark night with Jesus, reliving in memory with him a time when it was night.

For we know that there are, and will be, times for us when it is night. And during those times we hope and pray that Jesus will be with us when our only companions are in darkness (Ps 88:18).

WEDNESDAY OF HOLY WEEK

Passover

The feast of Passover was, and is, the great feast of the Jewish religion. It commemorates the time when the Lord God "passed over" the houses of the Hebrews, whose doorposts had been anointed with the blood of the sacrificed lamb prior to liberation from Egypt and the Exodus.

In the Synoptic Gospels, Jesus celebrates the Passover meal with his disciples. There is a jarring note that occurs during that meal: "…one of you will betray me" (Mt 26:21). This was hardly a topic for delightful dinner conversation. But this was no ordinary Passover supper. For, as soon becomes clear from the earliest and oldest strata of the Christian tradition, it was during this Passover meal that Jesus instituted the Eucharist: "This is my body. This is my blood."

The Eucharist anticipated the passion and death of Jesus: "…for this is my blood of the covenant, which is poured out for many for the forgiveness of sins" (Mt 26:28). But it is also a remembrance of this before the fact: "Do this in memory of me." As both anticipation and remembrance, the Eucharist weaves in and out of time, at least any ordinary understanding of time. And as if this were not paradoxical enough, the eucharistic rite hearkens back to an even more ancient past—the Hebrew Passover and the liberation of a people—and fast forwards to an event even farther in the future—a rite to be celebrated "until he comes."

In the Hebrew Passover, the doorpost in front of the house was sprinkled with blood so that the house would be passed over, unlike the houses of the Egyptians in which the first-born was slain. In the New Covenant established in the blood of the Lamb, it is we who are sprinkled with that blood so that we might be made to pass over into new life, into the freedom of the sons and daughters of God.

There was only one jarring note struck at the Passover meal hosted by Jesus before his passion and death. The rest of the meal was all harmony and peace.

HOLY THURSDAY

Foot Washing

Apparently, Jesus washed Judas's feet as well. It didn't seem to do any good—"...you are clean, though not all of you," said Jesus (Jn 13:10). Which means that the washing of the feet on the part of Jesus was not just about foot washing, but about something else. It was about being a part of Jesus, a part of what Jesus was doing with the foot washing, about what Jesus was doing with his life, serving and ministering to others. And Jesus urged the same loving service for his followers: "...you also should do as I have done to you" (Jn 13:15).

Service is not only about serving others, it is also about being served by others, allowing oneself to be served and graciously accepting the kindnesses of others. This is not always easy, especially if we prize our independence and do not like even the appearance of a dependence on others. To admit that we may need help is not always easy. Indeed, as we get older and, in fact, require more in the way of help and assistance than we may like to admit, we may even resent the proffered aid and support all the more.

Accepting the washing of one's feet, as Peter found out, can be almost as difficult, perhaps even more so, than actually doing the washing. At the end of the monastic liturgy on Holy Thursday, the abbot washes the feet (actually only the right foot) of a half dozen of the monks. The master of ceremonies tries to get different "volunteers" each year for variety's sake, but often ends up with the same people year after year. He gets a lot of refusals. Seemingly, there are a goodly number of "Peters" in the monastic community.

On the other hand, from the account in John's Gospel, Judas made no objection to having his feet washed by Jesus, even if it didn't do any good.

There are many things we don't understand in life, and still others that we understand all too well.

GOOD FRIDAY

Life and Death

It is not possible to write a complete autobiography. The final chapter is always missing. For we never know precisely where, when, or how the end of our life story will be played out. If diagnosed with a terminal illness or an incurable disease, we may have a fairly good idea, but never exactly.

There is a great deal about our birth that is just as fuzzy. We may be in possession of a birth certificate, indicating the time and the place of our birth, who our parents were, how much we weighed, and so forth. Our mother may have described our birth as easy or difficult. Still, although we were there of course for the event, we do not remember much—really, nothing—about this significant event in our lives.

So what is the meaning of a birth or a death? Are they simply bookends holding the chapters of a life in between? Both are more than that. A birth can be given an entirely new meaning by the life that is later lived, particularly if we become famous (or infamous). By the same token, the meaning of a death is always within the context of a life. For generally, we die as we live. As we have lived, so we die. There are deathbed conversions, but they cannot be counted on. If we wait until the last minute to turn our lives around, we may wait too long. At the end, we may be in no condition to effect it. Deathbed conversions, when they do occur, have generally been prepared for earlier in life so that one is, at least, open to such a possibility.

In the Letter to the Hebrews, it says that Christ offered prayers and supplications with loud cries and tears to God who was able to save him from death (Heb 5:7–9). The letter goes on to say that God heard his prayer. Well, yes and no. For Christ did, indeed, die. The Father did not save him from death, from the horrible death on a cross. Yet, Hebrews goes on to say that the Son learned obedience from what he suffered, and thus perfected, he became the source of eternal salvation for all who obey him.

A death, any death, gains meaning within the context of a life that is lived obediently to the call of the One who was obedient to the Father.

HOLY SATURDAY

Resurrection

"...and three days after being killed, he will rise again" (Mk 9:31). So said Jesus of the Son of Man.

Holy Saturday is a day of waiting—things are on hold. Jesus has died. And under the auspices of a pious Jew, Joseph of Arimathea, a respected member of the Sanhedrin, Jesus has been hastily buried. It would not do to have the body of a fellow Jew, albeit one convicted and executed for blasphemy, to be left hanging on the cross during Passover, the most solemn of Jewish feast days.

It took a certain amount of courage on Joseph's part to go to Pilate and ask for Jesus' body. Pilate was always in bad sorts during Jewish high holy days, what with the large number of pilgrims in the city and the potential for trouble. There is nothing quite like religion for getting people's dander up.

Mary Magdalene and Mary the mother of Joses saw where the body had been laid. They would come the day after the Sabbath, along with Salome, with aromatic oil and spices to give Jesus a proper Jewish burial.

However, they found no body.

They had been wondering how they would roll back the large stone that had been placed before the tomb. But it was already rolled back. A young man dressed in white tells them that Jesus of Nazareth whom they seek, the one who had been crucified, has been raised. Finally, they are told to tell his disciples that he will see them in Galilee.

91

But the women were so filled with fear and amazement from what they had experienced that they did not say anything to anyone. They fled.

Eventually, they must have told someone, above all after they encountered disciples who had seen the risen Lord.

Not that matters were any clearer even after that. And what were they to do with all the aromatic oil and spices?